Oh, the Wonders Ahead

EDITED BY SARAH ARAK

Oh, the Wonders Ahead
Copyright © 2006, Silverback Books, Inc.

All rights reserved. No part of this book may be used or reproduced in any manner whatsoever without prior written permission of the publisher.

Photographs courtesy of Jupiterimages.
Used with permission. All rights reserved.

Cover design by Richard Garnas
Interior design and production by Patty Holden

ISBN: 1-59637-078-5

Printed and bound in China

Introduction

AT ANY STAGE OF OUR EDUCATION, GRADUATION CAN BE ONE of the most exciting and uncertain times of our lives. Behind us lie years of hard work, persistence and dedication. Before us, however, the future is unknown. Thus, graduation is often a time of conflicting impulses; an emotional crossroads where we find ourselves caught between a desire to celebrate our past accomplishments and a need to a plan for the future.

Perhaps there is no way to reconcile this unique moment in life except to enjoy it. It is one of the few times in our lives when we can truly throw caution to the wind, and savor the feeling of success without being tainted by the fear of failure. Having come this far, anything is possible; having overcome so many obstacles, we are finally free to dream our own dreams.

Whatever the future may hold, one thing is certain—graduation, the moment of triumph, belongs to us forever. We may take our falls in life, but as long as we retain the will to get up and try again there is nothing to fear. Our graduations are proof that hard work is rewarded, and that good things truly come to those who persist.

Hitch your wagon to a star.

—Ralph Waldo Emerson

WHEN YOU LEAVE HERE,

DON'T FORGET WHY YOU CAME.

—Adlai Stevenson, to college graduates

AT COMMENCEMENT YOU WEAR YOUR SQUARE-SHAPED MORTARBOARDS. MY HOPE IS THAT FROM TIME TO TIME YOU WILL LET YOUR MINDS BE BOLD, AND WEAR SOMBREROS.

—Paul Freund

IF OPPORTUNITY DOESN'T KNOCK,

BUILD A DOOR.

—Milton Berle

Your families are extremely proud of you.

This would be a most opportune time

to ask for money.

—Gary Bolding

The roots of education are bitter,

but the fruit is sweet.

—Aristotle

REMEMBER TO THINK BIG THOUGHTS,

BUT RELISH SMALL PLEASURES.

—H. Jackson Brown, Jr.

THE FIREWORKS BEGIN TODAY.

EACH DIPLOMA IS A LIGHTED MATCH.

EACH ONE OF YOU IS A FUSE.

—Edward Koch

Stay hungry. Stay foolish.

—Steve Jobs, from a commencement speech
delivered at Stanford University on June 12, 2005,
quoting from the *Whole Earth Catalog*

A PERSON WHO HAS NEVER GONE TO SCHOOL MAY

STEAL FROM A FREIGHT CAR; BUT IF HE OR SHE

HAS A UNIVERSITY EDUCATION, HE OR SHE

MAY STEAL THE WHOLE RAILROAD.

—Theodore Roosevelt

You are educated. Your certification is in your degree.

You may think of it as the ticket to the good life.

Let me ask you to think of an alternative.

Think of it as your ticket to change the world.

—Tom Brokaw

OF COURSE, THERE'S A LOT OF KNOWLEDGE IN UNIVERSITIES.

THE FRESHMEN BRING A LITTLE IN;

THE SENIORS DON'T TAKE MUCH AWAY,

SO KNOWLEDGE SORT OF ACCUMULATES.

—A. Lawrence Lowell

THE LARGER THE ISLAND OF KNOWLEDGE,

THE LONGER THE SHORELINE OF WONDER.

—Ralph W. Sockman

There is a good reason they call these ceremonies 'commencement exercises.' Graduation is not the end; it's the beginning.

—Orrin Hatch

Success means having the courage,

the determination, and the will to become the

person you believe you were meant to be.

—George Sheehan

COMMENCEMENT SPEECHES WERE INVENTED LARGELY

IN THE BELIEF THAT OUTGOING COLLEGE STUDENTS

SHOULD NEVER BE RELEASED INTO THE WORLD

UNTIL THEY HAVE BEEN PROPERLY SEDATED.

—Garry Trudeau

An investment in knowledge always pays the best interest.

—Benjamin Franklin

It is clear the future holds great opportunities.
It also holds pitfalls. The trick will be to
avoid the pitfalls, seize the opportunities,
and get back home by six o'clock.

—Woody Allen,
"My Speech to the Graduates," Side Effects, 1980

WHEREVER YOU GO, NO MATTER WHAT THE WEATHER,

ALWAYS BRING YOUR OWN SUNSHINE.

—Anthony J. D'Angelo

Just about a month from now,

I'll be set adrift, with a diploma for

a sail and lots of nerve for oars.

✒

—Richard Halliburton

REMEMBER, IF YOU AREN'T FIRED WITH ENTHUSIASM,

YOU WILL BE FIRED WITH ENTHUSIASM!

—Vince Lombardi

It is not the mountain we conquer

but ourselves.

—Edmund Hillary

THERE ARE NO SHORTCUTS TO ANY

PLACE WORTH GOING.

—Beverly Sills

You cannot help but learn more as you take the

world into your hands. Take it up reverently,

for it is an old piece of clay,

with millions of thumbprints on it.

—John Updike

THE HEIGHT OF YOUR ACCOMPLISHMENTS

WILL EQUAL THE DEPTH OF

YOUR CONVICTIONS.

JP

—William F. Scolavino

We cannot direct your wind,

but we can adjust the sails.

—Author Unknown

YOUR SCHOOLING MAY BE OVER,

BUT REMEMBER THAT YOUR

EDUCATION STILL CONTINUES.

—Author Unknown

home $w\{X \le x\} = x$ SOEP

$\to$ ...

X_n: Anteil Einer...

$\ln(X_n) = \frac{1}{n} \sum (y_{ni} - \mu_{ni}) \frac{v(\mu_{ni})}{w_{ni}}$

MNC $\sum \frac{v^2(\mu_{ni})}{w_{ni}}$

O.K

1) Zusatzaufg. Wahrschein1.
2) Übung Wi-Statistik

$\sqrt{T}(\hat{\beta} - \beta)$ $\mu_{ni} = \begin{pmatrix} 2303 \\ 330\beta \end{pmatrix}$ $\begin{matrix} 33 \\ 133 \end{matrix}$

$var \frac{1}{T_2} = \ldots$

If you think education is expensive,

try ignorance.

—Andy McIntyre

BE WHO YOU ARE AND SAY WHAT YOU FEEL,

BECAUSE THOSE WHO MIND DON'T MATTER

AND THOSE WHO MATTER DON'T MIND.

—Dr. Seuss

Cherish your visions and your dreams.

They are the children of your soul,

the blueprints of your ultimate achievements.

—Napoleon Hill

NEVER WAS THERE A HORSE THAT COULDN'T BE RODE,

AN' THERE NEVER WAS A RIDER WHO

COULDN'T BE THROWED.

↪

—Louie L'Amour

It takes courage to grow up and become who you really are.

—e.e. cummings

Whatever you do, do it with

all your heart.

—Confucius

THERE IS JUST ONE LIFE FOR EACH OF US:

OUR OWN.

—Euripides

In the business world, everyone is paid in

two coins: cash and experience.

Take the experience first;

the cash will come later.

—Harold Geneen

Do not follow where the path may lead.

Go, instead, where there is no path

and leave a trail.

—Ralph Waldo Emerson

DON'T BE AFRAID TO TAKE A BIG STEP IF ONE IS INDICATED; YOU CAN'T CROSS A CHASM IN TWO SMALL JUMPS.

—David Lloyd George

The important thing is not

to stop questioning.

⚜

—Albert Einstein

WISE ARE THOSE WHO LEARN THAT THE

BOTTOM LINE DOESN'T ALWAYS HAVE

TO BE THEIR TOP PRIORITY.

—William Arthur Ward

WHAT LIES BEHIND US AND WHAT LIES BEFORE

US ARE TINY MATTERS COMPARED

TO WHAT LIES WITHIN US.

—Ralph Waldo Emerson

EXCELLENCE IS NOT A SKILL.

IT IS AN ATTITUDE.

— Ralph Marston

Don't live down to expectations.

Go out there and do

something remarkable.

—Wendy Wasserstein

PHOTO CREDITS

COVER PHOTO: Plush Studios; P. 5: Tanya Constantine; P. 6: Via Productions; P. 9: pbnj productions; P. 10: Rob Melnychuk; P. 13: Ibid; P. 14: Jack Hollingsworth; P. 17: Frare/Davis Photography; P. 18: Steven Puetzer; P. 21: Rob Melnychuk; P. 22: PNC; P. 25: Burke/Triolo Productions; P. 26: IVALO 140; P. 29: Anthony-Masterson; P. 30: Plush Studios; P. 33: trbfoto; P. 34: Plush Studios; P. 37: Tanya Constantine; P. 38: James Carroll; P. 41: es; P. 42: SW Productions; P. 45: Tony Baker; P. 46: SW Productions; P. 49: Jan Erik Posth; P. 50: C.F. Everest; P. 53: Maria Taglienti-Molinari; P. 54: Brian Hagiwara; P. 57: Jan Erik Posth; P. 58: Stephen Wisbauer; P. 61: SW Productions; P. 62: Ibid; P. 65: Rob Melnychuk; P. 66: Burke/Triolo Productions; P. 69: David Troncoso; P. 70: Maria Taglienti-Molinari; P. 73: Ibid; P. 74: SW Productions; P. 77: Plush Studios; P. 78: Elyse Lewin; P. 81: Edward Duarte; P. 82: es; P. 85: Rob Melnychuk; P. 86 SW Productions.

The beautiful photos you see throughout this book are courtesy of Jupiterimages.
For more information on the contributing photographers, visit www.jupiterimages.com.

jupiterimages.